GLOSSARY

Amphibious The ability to move or live both in water and on land.

Aquatic Living in water.

Blubber A thick layer of insulating fat that forms under the skin of sea mammals and polar bears.

Camouflage A pattern, color or body shape that helps an animal hide by blending in with its surroundings.

Carnivore An animal that eats flesh. Also, a member of the mammalian order Carnivora.

Convergent evolution The independent evolution of similar features in different animals, such as wings in bats and birds.

Echolocation Seeing by sound. Bats and dolphins echolocate by producing special sounds and analysing the echoes.

Herbivore An animal that mainly eats plant food.

Hibernation A type of very deep sleep in which an animal's body systems almost shut down to help it conserve energy.

Marsupial A type of mammal that gives birth to tiny young that develop further in a pouch, or attached to teats on the mother's belly.

Migration A long journey undertaken by animals to find food or a place to breed. Many animals migrate each year during certain seasons.

Monotreme A type of mammal that lays eggs.

Nocturnal Active at night.

Omnivore An animal that eats both plant foods and animal foods.

Placenta An internal organ that allows unborn mammals to absorb food and oxygen from the mother's bloodstream.

Primate A type of mammal with grasping hands, forward-facing eyes, and a large brain.

Prosimian A type of primate that is only distantly related to monkeys and apes. Most are small nocturnal creatures.

Rain forest A type of forest that gets heavy rain all year round. Tropical rain forests occur in tropical parts of the world; temperate rain forests occur in cooler places.

Rodent A type of mammal with sharp, chisel-like front teeth for gnawing.

Rumination Regurgitating food to chew it a second time. Ruminant animals have a special stomach containing bacteria that help them digest plant food.

Savanna Areas of grassland found in tropical regions.

Symbiosis A very close relationship between two different species.

Warm-blooded Having a relatively constant internal body temperature.

MAMMAL RECORDS

Biggest marine mammal Blue whale. Largest recorded length: 110 ft (33.5 m). Largest recorded weight: 193 tons (196 tonnes). Bigger examples may exist.

Biggest land mammal African elephant. Largest recorded length: 24 ft (7.3 m); height: 13 ft (4 m); weight: 13.5 tons (14.9 tonnes).

Tallest mammal Giraffe. Tallest recorded length: 20 ft (6 m).

Smallest mammal Bumblebee (Kitti's hog-nosed) bat. Head and body length: 1.1–1.3 in (27.9–33 mm).

Fastest land mammal Cheetah. Fastest speed recorded: 65 mph (105 kph).

Slowest land mammal Three-toed sloth. Speed in trees: 0.17 mph (0.27 kph).

Largest litter Common tenrec. Largest number recorded: 32 (30 survived), although normal litter size is 15.

Longest gestation period Indian elephant. Average period of 609 days (over 20 months) with a maximum period of 760 days (22 months).

Shortest gestation period American opossum (Virginian opossum) and rare water opossum (yapok). Average period of 12–13 days.

Longest migration (swimming) Gray whale. A round trip of 12,400 miles (20,000 km).

Deepest diver Sperm whale. Can probably reach depths of at least 2 miles (3.2 km).

Highest altitude Yak. Can climb to about 20,000 ft (6,000 m).

Loudest land mammal Howler monkey. Sound can be heard 3 miles (4.8 km) away.

Loudest sound produced Some baleen whales produce sounds that can travel all the way across entire oceans. The sound of blue whales and fin whales have been recorded at 188 decibels.

Smelliest mammal Striped skunk. Its smell contains seven major volatile and foul-smelling chemicals.

MAMMAL WEBSITES

| Rhino 50 yrs | Chimp 53 yrs | Hippo 54 yrs | Dolphin 65 yrs | Indian elephant 77 yrs |

Measuring Sizes

© Aladdin Books Ltd 1998
Produced by
Aladdin Books Ltd
28 Percy Street
London W1P OLD

First published in the United States
in 1998 by
Copper Beech Books,
an imprint of
The Millbrook Press
2 Old New Milford Road
Brookfield, Connecticut 06804

Project Editor: Sally Hewitt
Editor: Liz White
Design
David West Children's Book Design
Designer: Simon Morse
Photography: Roger Vlitos
Illustrator: Tony Kenyon

Printed in Belgium
5 4 3 2 1

Library of Congress Cataloging-in-Publication Data
King, Andrew, 1961-
Measuring sizes / by Andrew King ; illustrated by Tony Kenyon.
p. cm. — (Math for fun)
Includes index.
Summary: Combines games and projects to describe how to
measure length, area, and volume.
ISBN 0-7613-0853-9 (lib. bdg). — ISBN 0-7613-0747-8 (pbk.)
1. Mensuration—Juvenile literature. [1.Measurement.]
I. Kenyon, Tony, ill. II. Title.
III. Series: King, Andrew, 1961-
Math for fun.
QA465.K515 1998   98-4230
530.8'01—dc21   CIP AC

MATH *for fun*

Measuring Sizes

Andrew King

Copper Beech Books
Brookfield, Connecticut

CONTENTS

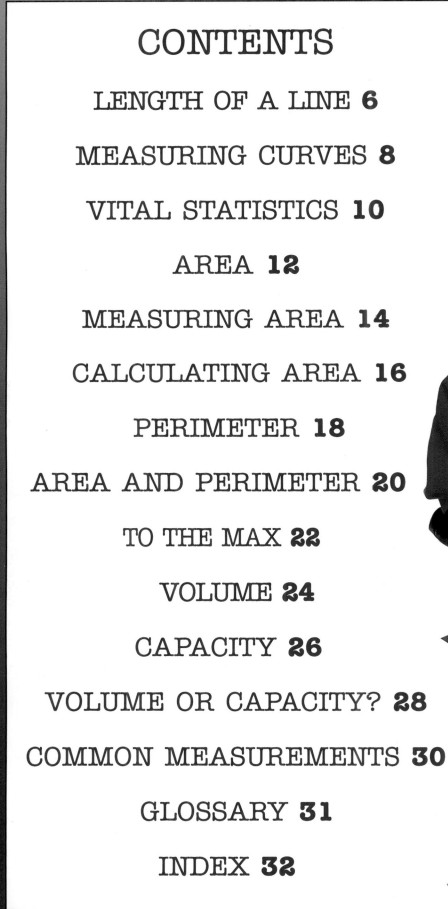

INTRODUCTION

Everywhere you look you will see lines, curves, and shapes of different lengths and sizes. But do you know how to measure them? Make a racecourse, construct your own skeleton, and have fun learning how to measure length, area, perimeter, volume, and capacity.

Try the exciting activities, practical projects, and fun games in this book, and you can learn about measuring sizes.

● Follow the STEP-BY-STEP INSTRUCTIONS to help you with the activities.

● Use the HELPFUL HINTS for clues about the experiments and games.

● Look at MORE IDEAS for information about other projects.

1 Yellow squares mean this is an easy activity.

2 Blue squares mean this is a medium activity.

3 Pink squares mean this is a more difficult activity. You'll have to think hard!

LENGTH OF A LINE

How tall are you? How high can you reach? To answer questions like these we need to measure length. People used to measure length by counting up the number of hand lengths... but everyone's hands are slightly different. Now most people use a **standard measurement** like feet to measure length.

MAKE A DERBY

Can your horse be first past the winning post?

1 Find a piece of cardboard. Fold it in half length-wise and cut it along the fold. Do the same again with another piece of cardboard and stick the four parts together to make one long strip.

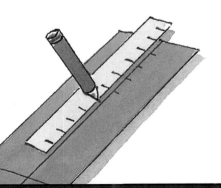

2 Starting from the bottom of the cardboard, use a ruler with inches to draw a straight line up the middle.

3 Mark in all the inch spaces on the line from one inch at the bottom to 12 inches, which makes one foot, at the top.

4 Now you can decorate it to look like a race course. Make a winning post from some cardboard and stand it at one end. Cut out two cardboard shapes of horses and riders and decorate them brightly.

HELPFUL HINTS

● To make a neat seam, turn over the cardboard. Place the strips next to each other, but not overlapping. Cover the seam with some tape. Now turn it over... a perfect finish!

5 Cut out a rectangle of thick cardboard for each horse to stand on. To make the horse stand up, attach it to the base with two pieces of play dough.

MORE IDEAS

● You can make the game even more fun by making some danger cards!

● If somebody throws a 1, they must pick up a card. The message might say "Horse frightened by mouse, miss a turn" or how about "High fence, go back 4in!"

6 Place your horses at the start and take turns to roll the die and move your horse forward. The first past the post wins!

MEASURING CURVES

The difficult thing with rulers is that they are always straight. Unfortunately, most of the world isn't. In fact, it is wonderful how wiggly and bendy the world is. Without bumps and curves the world would be a far less interesting place! So, how can you go about measuring them?

WIGGLY WORMS

How good are your friends at guessing the right length of straight lines? What about wiggly lines? Make some wiggly worms to find out!

1 Find some string or thick colored cord and measure out some different lengths against a ruler. You could cut lengths of 2, 4, 6, and 8 inches.

2 Stick the lengths of string in a wiggly line on pieces of cardboard. These will be your worms. Now draw around each worm on the cards and decorate each worm to look really slimy!

3 Write the length of each worm on the back of the cards so you don't forget.

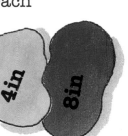

4 Challenge your friends to guess the length of each worm. The person that makes the nearest guess is the winner!

HELPFUL HINTS

● If some of your friends find it hard to make a good guess, you could show them how to use a "rule of thumb" to help. Strangely enough, with this "rule of thumb" you use your little finger! Most little fingers are about 0.25in wide so you can use it to move along the back of the worm to estimate its length.

MORE IDEAS

● Why don't you try estimating the length of edges! If you have got some old vegetables, cut them in half and draw around the edge on a piece of paper. Guess how long each edge is and write it down.

● You can find out how long the edge really is by using some string to match along the edge of the outline and mark off the length. Next, straighten the string and measure its length against a ruler and check to see how close you really were!

VITAL STATISTICS

"You have grown so tall!" Whenever you meet someone who hasn't seen you for a while it's usually the first thing they say. Sometimes, people call measurements of the body the **vital statistics**. You need to know yours to find clothes that will fit and comfortable shoes.

SKELETONS

You can make a skeleton to show your vital statistics!

1 Find some cardboard and cut it up into long strips.

2 Measure from the base of your neck to your hips with a tape measure. Tape some strips together to match the measurement. This will be the backbone. Write this on the strip so you don't forget.

3 Now measure the width of your hips. Cut a strip to match and attach it to the other strip with a butterfly pin. Put the pin through both pieces of paper and bend the arms back. Ask an adult to help you with this.

4 Measure other parts of your body and pin them all on to make your skeleton! How many parts can you include? What about your fingers and toes?

HELPFUL HINTS

● You could draw a stick figure first to show the parts of your body you are going to measure. As you measure each part, write it down on the stick figure picture.

● You can then cut all the strips of cardboard to the right length and join them together. You could make some strips thicker to make your skeleton more realistic.

● You can add a skull to your skeleton by measuring around your head with a tape measure. Make a strip to match the length, loop it over, and stick it together.

● Do the same again, measuring around your head from top to bottom. Loop the strip around and stick it to the first skull loop.

● Make a bright face from pieces of cardboard and stick this onto the head with tape.

AREA

Have you ever had new tiles put into your bathroom or kitchen? We call the space you want to cover, the **area**. Often the tiles are square shaped and this is how the size of an area is measured — in squares.

TILE FLIPPING

To win this game you need to capture the area covered by the tiles by flipping all the squares over to your color.

1 Find two pieces of different colored cardboard the same size. Stick them together back to back. Draw a square grid on the cardboard with lines about 1in apart. The squares will be your tiles.

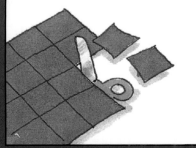

2 Cut out 16 tiles. Now you are ready to play the game.

3 Turn the tiles so that eight are showing red and eight are green. Arrange them in a square.

4 The first player is the green team. He rolls a die. If a 3 is rolled, then three cards are turned over from red to green.

HELPFUL HINTS

● When you stick the cardboard together make sure you cover the whole sheet with a thin layer of glue. If you don't, some of the tiles might fall apart when they are cut into squares.

5 Now it is the red player's turn. He has one throw and turns back the number of cards shown on the die from green to red.

MORE IDEAS

● To play Tile Flipping you arranged the 16 square tiles to make a bigger square shape. What other numbers of tiles can you find that can be arranged to make a square? You could try four tiles, but there are others, too. These are special numbers that are called square numbers!

6 The die is then passed back and the battle to win all sixteen squares continues until one of the players captures them all!

MEASURING AREA

Like measuring length, not everything in the world comes in straight lines or simple squares that are easy to count and measure. Most areas that need measuring come in all sorts of unusual shapes.

BIG FOOT?
What do you think covers the greatest area, your foot or your hand? Take a quick look at them and press one against the other.

1 Draw a grid of squares on a piece of paper with your ruler. Helpful Hints tells you how to do this if you are stuck.

2 Place one of your feet on the grid and get a friend to draw around it with a bright marker. Color in the shape of the foot so you can see it clearly.

3 Do the same again on another grid with your hand.

4 To find the area of the foot, count all the whole squares inside the print.

but not one like this.

5 Next, count all the squares that are more than half covered by the print. You would count a square like this...

6 What is the total area covered by your foot? Now count the squares covered by your hand. Which is the largest?

HELPFUL HINTS

● To make the grid of squares, line your ruler up with the edge of the paper and draw a straight line. Move the ruler along the paper so that the edge is now resting on the line you have just drawn. Draw a new line and repeat this across the page. Do the same moving across the page in the other direction like this to make the squares.

MORE IDEAS
● Why don't you find out the area covered by your mom or dad's foot?
● Make a guess and then find out. But watch out, they may have smelly feet!

CALCULATING AREA

You can't always find the area of something by counting squares! Sometimes, it is easier to calculate area by using multiplication tables. If you need to find the area of a rectangle all you need to do is multiply the length by the width. So, for a rectangle that has sides of 2in and 4in the area is 2in x 4in = 8 **square inches**!

AREA ARITHMETIC
To be good at this game your friends will need good estimation skills and a good memory for number facts.

 Plan some rectangles to draw on a piece of scrap paper.

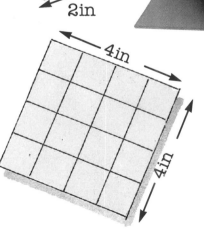

5in

2in

 The first one might be 2in long and 4in wide, so the area would be 2in x 5in = 10 square inches.

4in

4in

3 The second might be 4in long and 4in wide, so the area would be 4in x 4in = 16 square inches. It is easy to see if you mark off the squares.

4 Make about ten different rectangles and draw them on cardboard. Don't mark in the individual squares. Mark each rectangle with a letter. Write the answers on a piece of paper and hide it from your friend.

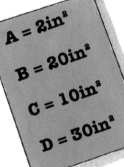

A = 2in²
B = 20in²
C = 10in²
D = 30in²

HELPFUL HINTS

● To make it easier for some of your friends to play, you could draw a square inch on the corner of each card to help them with their estimates.

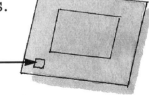

1 square inch ——⟶

5 Now, challenge your friends to estimate the area of each of the rectangles. The person who estimates most accurately wins!

MORE IDEAS

● Have you noticed that some rectangles look different but have the same area!

● A rectangle with sides of 3in and 6in and one with sides 9in and 2in long both have the same area because 3in x 6in = 18 square inches and 2in x 9in = 18 square inches.

● Make up a new quiz. This time make all the rectangles different shapes but the same area. Do you think your friends will notice your trick?

PERIMETER

The **perimeter** of a shape is the line that goes around its edge. It is quite easy to figure out the perimeter of some shapes with straight edges. You can measure the length of each edge with a ruler then add up the lengths to find the total. The lengths of each side of this triangle are 3in, 4in, and 5in. The total length is 3in + 4in + 5in = 12in.

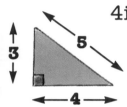

STRING SHAPES
This is a fun way of making lots of strange and unusual shapes that all have the same perimeter length.

1 Measure out a piece of string about three feet long. Join the ends of the string with a piece of tape like this.

2 Find a large piece of paper and put the string on it. Now, arrange the string to make an interesting shape. Make sure the string doesn't loop over itself.

3 Now, draw close to the outside edge of the string lightly with a pencil. Take the string away and paint the area on the inside of the perimeter your favorite color.

4 Now, paint the outside a different color. Wait until the paint dries and then go over the perimeter again with a thick black marker to make it stand out.

5 Try making a new shape with the same piece of string — something that looks completely different. The perimeter will still be the same!

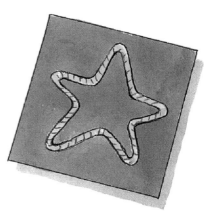

6 Whatever shape you have made with the string, the perimeter will always be three feet!

HELPFUL HINTS
● To make it easier to draw around the string on the paper without it moving, you could stick down parts of it with some play dough.

MORE IDEAS
● Can you make all the letters of your name in turn with the three-foot piece of string as the perimeter?

● You could make each letter on a separate piece of paper then decorate them to make them look colorful.

AREA AND PERIMETER

The perimeter goes all the way around a shape. The inside of the shape is called the area. Some shapes have the same area, but the length of the perimeter might be longer or shorter, it doesn't always stay the same.

SQUARE SHUFFLING
Can you shuffle eight squares to make the longest possible perimeter?

1 When you have made eight square cards try an arrangement. One side of each square must touch one side of at least one other square.

2 If you arranged the cards like this, the perimeter would be 14 sides long.

3 What is the longest perimeter you can make?

4 If you think you have found the longest perimeter try to find the shortest!

HELPFUL HINTS

● A quick way of making a square from a piece of cardboard is to gently fold over one of the corners to touch the side edge and then make a mark where it meets. Then fold over the end to that mark and make a sharp crease like this. Cut along the crease and you have a square.

Cut along crease

MORE IDEAS

● You can make the longest perimeter in lots of different ways. Here is one way of doing it.

● Did you find any others? Can you see how arrangements of squares that give the longest perimeter are similar? They all spread out the squares so that as many edges as possible of each square are part of the perimeter.

● Now you know this rule, can you quickly find a shape with twelve squares with the longest perimeter possible? It should have a perimeter 26 sides long. What would be the longest perimeter you could make if you used 24 squares?

TO THE MAX

One problem mathematicians often face is how to get the **maximum** out of something. Knowing how to find the maximum amount of area when the perimeter has to stay the same is very useful for solving lots of practical problems.

THE FARMER'S FENCE
Can you help the farmer to fix his fences so that he can make as much space for his chickens as possible?

1 The farmer is poor and can only afford 16 panels of fencing. The fences will only join together in a straight line or at right angles.

2 The farmer decides to make a plan. You could use old burned matches, **but make sure you ask an adult first.**

3 He started by laying out the fences like this. The area inside the perimeter of the fence is ten squares.

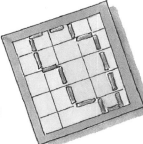

He tries again. This time the area is worse! Only nine squares.

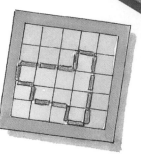

Can you find a better way of arranging the perimeter fencing to make the greatest possible area for the farmer's chickens?

HELPFUL HINTS

● You might find it easier to figure out the area if you draw out a grid to put your matches on.

● Put a match you are using for the fence on the corner of a piece of paper and make a mark like this.

● Move it down the side of the paper making marks along the edge. Do the same along each side of the paper.

● Now join the marks across the page with a ruler and pencil.

MORE IDEAS

● Things have been looking up on the farm! The farmer has made some extra money and can now afford four new panels of fencing.

● What is the maximum area he can make for the fence now?

VOLUME

You might have heard your mom or dad suggest that you "turn the volume down and play quietly!" When mathematicians use the word **volume** they are not talking about the amount of sound that is made. The volume of a shape is the amount of space it takes up. It is often measured in **cubed inches**.

MAKIN' AND SHAPIN'
Can you shape a cube of play dough into amazing monsters?

1 First of all, try making one a cubed inch. Draw a square inch on a piece of paper as above.

2 Roll some play dough into a ball. Use two rulers to squash the sides until it fits the square. Keep doing this to all the sides until you have made a cube. You might have to add more dough or take some away to make each side of the cube fit the square.

3 Now you have made a cubed inch it doesn't matter what you do to it, squash it, pinch it or push a hole through it — it will always be one cubed inch.

4 But one cubed inch is a little small. Draw out a square 5in by 5in. This makes an area of 5in x 5in = 25 square inches.

5 When you have made this larger cube it will be 5in x 5in x 5in = 125 cubed inches. You can make some amazing monsters with a volume of this size!

HELPFUL HINTS

● Remember that the volume will only stay the same size if you keep all the play dough together.

● If you start to take pieces off the volume will be smaller. If you add pieces on it will become larger.

MORE IDEAS

● It is amazing how large the volume of some small shapes can be.

● To find the volume of a cube you have to multiply the length of the edge by itself and then once more. So, the volume of a cube that has edges 2in long would be 2in x 2in x 2in = 8 cubed inches. What is the volume of a cube with edges of 10in? What about 99in? You may need a calculator to figure out this one.

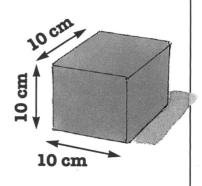

10 cm
10 cm
10 cm

CAPACITY

A ten-gallon hat was meant to have the **capacity** to hold ten gallons of water! Capacity is the way we measure the amount of substance a container will hold.

FILL IT UP!

How good are you at estimating the amount of water you need to fill up different containers?

1 Ask an adult if you can borrow some different empty containers like bottles and cups from the kitchen. Now find an old bottle top and get a large jug of water.

2 How many full bottle tops of water do you think it will take to fill up the cup for example?

3 Write down all the different containers on a score card and make an estimate of the number of full bottle tops you think each one will hold.

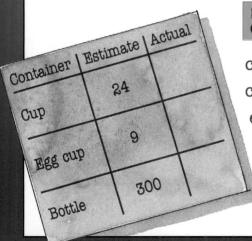

Container	Estimate	Actual
Cup	24	
Egg cup	9	
Bottle	300	

4 Now try filling the cup carefully. How many can it take before the water spills over the top? Write the total down on the scorecard. The person who makes the best estimate is the winner.

HELPFUL HINTS

● This can be quite a wet and messy game! It is a good idea to do the filling or pouring over a sink. If it is easier on a table put a towel down and place the containers on it to save everyone from getting soaked!

MORE IDEAS

● Ask an adult if you can borrow a measuring jug from the kitchen.

● You can play a similar game with cups. Fill a cup up to the brim and tip all the water into the jug. If you look on the side of the jug, you can see the measuring marks. These might be in fluid ounces, marked fl.oz., pints, marked pt., or gallons, marked gal. See if you can estimate how far up the measuring jug the water from a different size cup will go when you pour it in. How accurate can you make your estimates?

VOLUME OR CAPACITY?

Volume and capacity are similar. Volume is the amount of space occupied by an object and capacity refers to the amount of substance a container can hold. The capacity of a bottle holding 16 fl.oz does not change, but if you gulp some of the drink the volume of liquid is less.

WATER MUSIC

Some musical instruments make use of different volumes of air to make different notes. You can make your own bottle orchestra.

1 Ask an adult if you can borrow a glass bottle and a measuring jug. Tap the bottle with a pencil and listen to the sound it makes.

2 Try pouring in different volumes of water. Perhaps 8 fl.oz first.

3 Tap the outside of the bottle with a pencil. How has the sound changed? Yes! it is a higher note. Try 16 fl.oz., then 24 fl.oz. How is the sound affected now?

4 Try gathering some other glass bottles and make each have a different note. Can you make up a tune?

HELPFUL HINTS

● It is easier if you use bottles that are exactly the same. When you have found the amount of water in the bottle that gives you the note you want you can keep a record of what you have done by tipping all the water back into the measuring jug and writing down the amount.

● Take a look at the number of fluid ounces you used and write it down, so when you play your composition for bottles and orchestra you will know exactly how much to pour into each container!

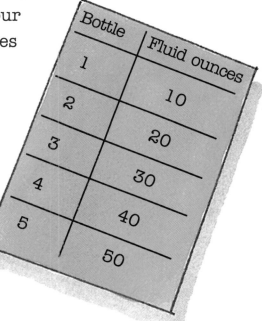

Bottle	Fluid ounces
1	
2	10
3	20
4	30
5	40
	50

COMMON MEASUREMENTS

AREA

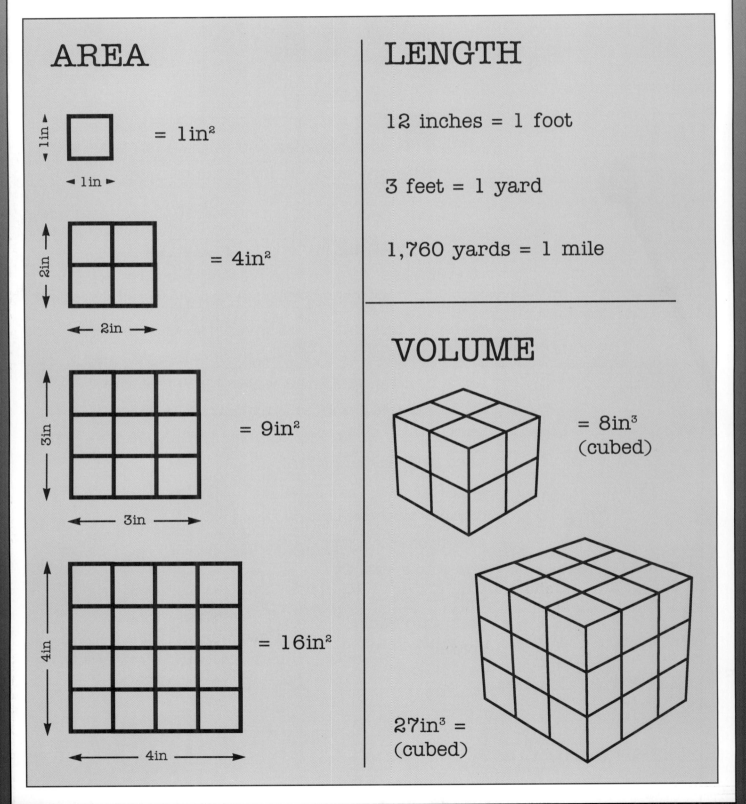

1in | 1in = 1in²

2in | 2in = 4in²

3in | 3in = 9in²

4in | 4in = 16in²

LENGTH

12 inches = 1 foot

3 feet = 1 yard

1,760 yards = 1 mile

VOLUME

= 8in³ (cubed)

27in³ = (cubed)